ANNABELLA'S BEDTIME BLESSING

Based on story idea by

LAURIYANA MOORE

with help from mom, **AYANNA LYNNAY**

Annabella 's Bedtime Blessing

Copyright © April 2024

Based on story idea by Lauriyana Moore

and Ayanna Lynnay

Published in the United States of America by

www.cb-publishing.com

ISBN: 978 - 1 - 945377 - 35 - 8

ANNABELLA'S BEDTIME BLESSING

Based on story idea by

LAURIYANA MOORE

with help from mom, **AYANNA LYNNAY**

Annabella and her mom, Alisha and her dad Mark, lived in a warm, cozy house in Buffalo, NY. They loved their home very much. Mark was a truck driver who had to go away often on long trips. Alisha was a nurse who helped many people. Annabella was a second-grader who loved to learn and play

Every morning, Annabella and Alisha walked to school together because it was close to their home and on the way to the hospital where Alisha worked. They liked to talk about many things during their walk, like the clouds, the trees, and what Annabella looked forward to doing at school.

One bright and sunny morning, Alisha noticed that Annabella seemed very tired. She gently asked, "You look sleepy. Did you have trouble sleeping last night?"

Annabella nodded, trying not to yawn. "Yes, Mom. I couldn't fall asleep," she admitted.

Alisha stopped and knelt, giving Annabella a comforting hug. "Let's make tonight different," she said with a smile. "After dinner, we'll have a special bedtime routine. A warm bath, a big hug, and a kiss goodnight. I'll even read your favorite bedtime story. I promise you'll sleep much better."

Annabella's eyes lit up at the thought. "Can we read the story about the brave little mouse?" she asked excitedly.

"Of course, my dear," Alisha replied, happy to see her daughter's spirits lift.

Annabella felt a little better as they continued their walk to school, thinking about the special bedtime routine. She was already looking forward to it.

That night, Alisha kept her promise. After a warm bath and getting into her pajamas, Annabella snuggled into bed, ready for the story. Alisha read about the brave little mouse's adventures, and Annabella listened, her eyes growing heavier with each page. When the story ended, Alisha gave Annabella a big hug and a kiss on the forehead. "Sweet dreams, my love," she whispered.

Annabella smiled, feeling cozy and loved. As her mom turned off the light, Annabella closed her eyes, feeling peaceful and ready for a good night's sleep.

Annabella tried very hard to sleep. She lay on her left side, then her right, on her tummy, and even on her back. She closed her eyes tight, hoping sleep would come. But it did not. Annabella even played a game, pretending to sleep, thinking it might help. But she still stayed awake

The night was long and too quiet. Annabella was very tired. She wanted to sleep because she had school in the morning. But sleep did not come.

When the morning light came into her room, Annabella got out of bed. Just then, her mom came in. "You are up early," her mom said.

"Good morning, Mom," Annabella said. She tried to smile but felt so tired

"Good morning, Annabella. You look very tired. Did you sleep well?" her mom asked.

"No, Mom. I still could not sleep," Annabella said.

"Why not? Our special bedtime plan did not work?" Mom asked.

"No Mom. It did not. I keep thinking about things that make me worried," Annabella said. She did not feel happy.

Her mom gave her a big hug. "You don't have to worry, my dear," her mom said. "Let's talk about what makes you worried. It might help. We can even call your dad to tell him all about it too."

Annabella felt a little better. Talking to her mom and her dad always made things seem okay. Her dad was big and strong and would not let anything happen to her. Her dad said he would be home on Monday morning and would bring her a special gift that she

After a long day, Annabella was very tired. She tried her best at school. She listened to her teachers and did all her work. Even though she was sleepy, she made it through the day. She really hoped she would sleep well at night. She was getting worried that she would never be able to sleep again! This made her even more worried and upset because she often heard her teachers say how important it was to get a good night's sleep if the students wanted to do good in school

Annabella wanted to do good in school but how could she if she did not get a good night's sleep?

Finally, it was bedtime. Annabella remembered something. "Mom, didn't we read that lavender helps you sleep?" she asked as they prepared for bed.

"Yes, we did," her mom said with a smile. "I'll put some lavender near your pillow to help you sleep." Her mom got the lavender and sprinkled some close to Annabella

"Good night, my dear," her mom said, giving her a kiss. Annabella smelled the sweet lavender and soon fell asleep. But after an hour, she woke up again. She started to worry about things, and she couldn't sleep anymore. Even the lavender didn't help her now.

The night was long, and Annabella only slept for a little bit. In the morning, she was very sleepy again. Her mom saw this and said, "It's okay. We'll find a new way to help you sleep. If it's still hard to sleep, we might visit Dr. Arnet." Annabella liked Dr. Arnet a lot. She is a special kind of nurse who can do doctor things too. Annabella's mom says she is a nurse practitioner. Annabella thinks she might want to be a nurse practitioner when she grows up.

But Annabella remembers getting a shot from Dr. Arnet, and it hurt. She worries if she might need a shot to help her sleep. She really hopes tonight will be better, so she doesn't need to get a shot.

Even though she was sleepy, Annabella tried to have a good day. She listened to her teachers and did her work, but she wasn't feeling happy. She was too tired to enjoy things that usually make her smile.

That night, her mom had a new idea. "Let's hope this works," said Annabella, not sure if it would.

"Don't worry, Annabella. I've heard that warm milk with a little honey can help," her mom said with a smile. They ate yummy cookies and drank warm milk with honey. Annabella felt sleepy after drinking her milk.

She said goodnight and went to bed.
After cleaning up, her mom checked on Annabella and saw her sleeping well. But, after a few hours, Annabella woke up. She tried and tried to sleep again but couldn't.

"You look sleepy, the milk didn't help much?" her mom said the next morning.
Annabella nodded. It was Saturday, no school today. Her mom said, "Have some breakfast and then relax. Maybe you can nap on the couch." Annabella had pancakes with chocolate on top and drank a glass of milk.

She tried to nap on the couch, but sleep just wouldn't come. Her mom was getting worried. She played some soft music, but that didn't help Annabella sleep either.

Nothing was working. That night, her mom had a new idea. "How about a warm bubble bath with the lights turned low?" Her mom got the bath ready and dimmed the lights. Annabella sat in the warm water, feeling calm. She really hoped this would help her sleep. But, even this didn't help her fall asleep much

The next morning was Sunday. Annabella was very, very tired. It was hard to get ready for church because she felt so sleepy. But she and her mom made it to church on time. Annabella loved going to her church Tabernacle of Praise. It was so much fun and she always learned something new about God.

That day, Pastor Charles talked about saying thank you to God. He told everyone it's very important to remember all the good things God does for us and to thank Him. Annabella listened and had a new idea. She realized she hadn't asked God to help her sleep. Maybe she was too busy trying to fix it quickly and forgot she could ask God for help.

That night, Annabella knew what she needed to do before bed. She told her mom, "Let's pray and thank God, and ask Him to help me sleep." Together, they prayed and started by saying thank you. "Dear God, thank you for my amazing mom and dad, the yummy food we have, my warm bed, my fun school, my nice teachers, and my great friends. Thank you for protecting my dad when he is driving his truck on the road and for keeping me and mom safe when he is gone. Thank you for helping me with everything," she prayed

Then, Annabella asked God to help her to get a good sleep. After praying, her mom gave her a kiss goodnight. Lying in bed, Annabella felt calm as she thought about all the blessings in her life. She wasn't worried anymore. Instead, she felt really happy

The next morning, Annabella woke up feeling happy and rested, so different from before. She was surprised how asking God for help made such a big change. She learned an important lesson about being thankful and praying. She learned that being thankful and praying can take away worrying. Annabella also learned another important lesson. It is always best to ask God for help first before trying stuff that may not work.

LAURIYANA'S PRAYER

Dear God, we thank you for allowing us to learn more about you. The more we learn about you the more we trust and rely on you. Help us to remember that you can help us with everything that we go through. Everything that may seem hard to do we know that you can help us. And we thank you for that. We pray that you help us to trust you even more so that we go to you first. In Jesus' name, we say Amen!

MEET LAURIYANA AND AYANNA

Lauriyana Moore is a 10-year-old 5th grader who lives in Buffalo, NY. She loves God, her family, cheerleading, gymnastics, and math. Lauriyana shares a special relationship with her dad, Lawrence, who is a pastor, and her mom, Ayanna, who is also a preacher. Lauriyana has a sweet spirit, and to know her is to love her. She loves Jesus and prays powerfully.

Lauriyana is very excited to have worked on this book with her mom!

Ayanna Lynnay is a minister, nurse, author, and book publisher. This is the first children's book published through her company, ChosenButterfly Publishing.

LAURIYANA & MOM AYANNA

Made in United States
North Haven, CT
04 May 2024